BUS SCENE IN COLOUR:
TEN YEARS OF DEREGULATION

STEPHEN MORRIS

IAN ALLAN Publishing

First published 1996

ISBN 0 7110 2493 6

Published by Ian Allan Publishing

an imprint of Ian Allan Ltd,
Terminal House, Station Approach,
Shepperton, Surrey TW17 8AS.
Printed by Ian Allan Printing Ltd,
Coombelands House, Coombelands Lane,
Addlestone, Surrey KT15 1HY

Front cover:
In the era of regulation, Midland Red was the proud giant amongst British bus companies. In later years it was split into four. At the time an audacious little Scottish independent was coming to people's notice; that company, Stagecoach, is now the proud giant of a new era — and owns the southern quarter of what was Midland Red. One of its standard Alexander-bodied Volvo B10Ms is seen in Coventry. *John Robinson*

Title page:
Stevensons was the sort of independent for which deregulation was tailor-made; it expanded rapidly by acquisition and also made sorties into new areas. It bought new buses when it could — like this Alexander-bodied Scania N113 — and also bought a lot of secondhand vehicles. One thing that deregulation hasn't improved is Birmingham's Bull Ring bus station; it is still quite unfit for human habitation. Stevensons is no longer independent; it is now part of Cowies, as is the Midland Red North Olympian behind. *John Robinson*

Introduction

Deregulation of bus services came about in October 1986, as a result of a Transport Act passed the previous year. This was designed to free the bus industry from 'the shackles' of 50 years of regulated bus services. At its best, deregulation was expected to unleash a new spirit of entrepreneurialism into the bus industry. There would be innovation right, left and centre; quality would soar, fares would drop, 'the market would provide' and we would all be happy.

What happened by and large was that operators stopped buying new buses, other than converted vans, which were unkindly referred to as bread vans. (They weren't bread vans at all; they were parcel vans...) They were painted in pretty colours to disguise their utilitarian nature, though they played their part in reducing running costs, improving frequencies and opening up places too cramped for 'real' buses. Much of the innovation naturally came from newcomers to the market who were promptly squashed by bigger operators protecting their patch from intruders. Fares didn't come down, but the quality did. Timetables changed rapidly, passengers got confused and stayed away, and competition on the road usually meant two or more operators running the same routes at the same time, rather than actually improving frequencies.

Now, 10 years on, we are clawing our way back. The industry is undoubtedly much more efficient than it was, and services don't continue to run where the passengers aren't, just because they have run there for donkey's years. Bus priority schemes are beginning to become more commonplace with new technology creeping in to information and fare-collection systems and improving accessibility. Investment in new buses is beginning to flow, even if the result is to squeeze too many passengers into buses which are too small; locally our ancient Leyland Nationals are at last going, replaced by new Dennis Darts which are swift, quiet, don't crash and bang like the Nationals did and have seats crammed so close together that I find them difficult to use! Such is progress...

However, public transport is climbing the political agenda — maybe not as quickly as it should, but it is climbing. Government has been making noises about introducing a measure of regulation if operators don't do better. The greatest excesses are over; the poorest-quality operators have done their worst and are disappearing, unable to fund asset replacement, keep on top of maintenance or resist pressure from bigger operators to give up or sell up. Timetables have become more stable and passenger decline is being stemmed at last. The bus, it seems, has a bright future.

In the meantime, though, we shall just enjoy a glance at the deregulated scene. As editor of *Buses,* I see lots of superb pictures which don't necessarily fit in with what we may be doing in the magazine, and then the moment passes. So this book gives a chance for just a few of them to see the light of day. As a result you will not be treated to a

...rned treatise on the application of ...onetarist theory in the field of mass ...blic transportation. Neither will you ...e any of my photos; this is really a ...bute to the photographers throughout ...e country who make *Buses* magazine ...ssible. And of course you won't see ...y London buses; London has not yet ...en subjected to the benefits of ...regulation, and has seen an increase ... passengers. Not that any value ...dgement is intended in the ...xtaposition of those two statements, ... course.

...What you will see is a slightly ragged ...ur of Britain, starting in Scotland ...veryone else seems to start in ...uthern England, so we'll be ...rverse!), trundling down the east ...de, along the bottom, back up the ...est, a quick side trip to 'Middle ...gland', then we'll take in Wales, a bit ... the northwest and then finish up in ...e West Midlands as we missed them ...t on the way up. You will see that the ...s is alive and well, and whether you ...e deregulation or not, at least the ...ene is so much more colourful and ...ried than it was in the 'good old days' ... 20 years ago. I hope you like it!

Stephen Morris, B. Mus, MCIT,
Addlestone, Surrey,
May 1996

...anks are due to my colleague ...dy Izatt who supplied some of the ...otos and has otherwise helped out ...th this book, and to all the ...otographers whose work is featured. ...ecial thanks are due to Tony Moyes, ...hose superb Welsh photos were ...companied by full and informative ...ptions, which saved me the job of ...aking them up.

Above:
The one name which has pervaded all things throughout the period of deregulation is Stagecoach, a child of the 1980s if ever there was one. Starting as a small coach operator, with an almost audacious outlook on life, to take advantage of coach deregulation which began on 6 October 1980, it took the opportunities of privatisation and deregulation in a shameless way. It became the biggest private bus group in the world, running on four continents: now running trains in Britain, trams in Portugal (after a fashion) and trolleybuses in New Zealand, and quoted on the London stock market. Perth is where it all started; this series B Leyland National began life with Ribble, another Stagecoach company, and is seen in September 1989 running for Perth Panther. *Andy Izatt*

Above:
With a distinct list to port, an ex-Eastern Counties Plaxton Supreme
IV-bodied Leyland Leopard, JVF 819V, of Galson Motors, Barvas, works
a local service on Lewis, to Stornoway from Carloway via Callanish, in
July 1995. *Andy Izatt*

Right:
Western Scottish expanded its operations to various Scottish islands
before becoming part of Stagecoach. In Western's post-privatisation,
pre-Stagecoach, black, white, grey and red livery, is an ex-British Airways
Leyland National, 704 (OIW 7024) on Rothesay in May 1995. Strathclyde
PTE operations tend to be identified with Greater Glasgow, but extended
well beyond that area into places where a PTE — usually associated with
urban conurbations — seemed rather inappropriate. *John Young*

Above:
Grampian Region Transport was the first Scottish bus company to be privatised and quickly grew to be a group in its own right, the impetus coming from the privatisation of the Scottish Bus Group in 1990. It developed its own style, aiming for a high-quality image which involved some distinctive vehicle purchases. In service with SMT (latterly Eastern Scottish) in Edinburgh is an all-singing, all-dancing Wright-bodied

Mercedes-Benz O.405 with double glazing and air conditioning. SMT, a long-established and respected name in Scottish bus circles, formally ceased to be during 1996, its operations split between Lowland — ironically a company formed out of Eastern Scottish in 1985 — and Midland, both adjoining FirstBus companies. SMT is retained as a trading name, however. *Richard Walter*

Above:

Deregulation effectively came early to Glasgow. The main operators saw little point in waiting for the witching hour, 26 October 1986, and licensed their new services from the end of August. Chaos reigned. Both Clydeside and Kelvin saw the Routemaster as a useful warhorse, although it needed a crew of two, it was nimble in traffic and could load much more quickly than a one-person bus, giving distinct competitive advantages. They were, moreover, cheap both to buy and to run — though neither company had a fantastic reputation for the maintenance of its Routemasters, as subsequent purchasers were to find to their cost. Seen in central Glasgow early on in the deregulation era — 15 November 1986 — are Clydeside's RM956 and an unidentified Kelvin bus. *Andy Izatt*

Left:
Stagecoach started in Glasgow as Magicbus at deregulation, also using Routemasters. It later sold the business — along with some buses — to Kelvin Central (as Kelvin had become), not before using one of its Megadekka 110-seat Hong Kong-style three-axle Leyland Olympians on the operation. F110 NES later went to East Midland and is now (1996) with United Counties. *Andy Izatt*

Right:
During 1992 Strathclyde Buses suffered a major fire at its Larkfield depot, resulting in numerous odd secondhand acquisitions entering the fleet for a time. Caught in rush-hour traffic in central Glasgow on 17 October 1992 is LA1452 (OTO 566M), an ex-Nottingham Northern Counties-bodied Leyland Atlantean. *John Allison*

Above:

Lowland Scottish was created out of the 1985 reorganisation of the Scottish Bus Group. It looked an unpromising operation, but managed to present a smart image and keep up with fleet replacement. It is now part of the FirstBus group, having been bought by GRT. Four Alexander (Belfast) Q-type-bodied Leyland Tigers were diverted to it from a big order for Ulsterbus — much to Leyland's chagrin — as the Ulsterbus Tiger, with its Volvo engine, was a special animal for that operator and not intended for general consumption. 303 (J303 ASH), seen in Langholm in April 1992, is a good-looking bus though.

John Young

Above:
Hartlepool Transport was privatised by sale to its employees, but after Stagecoach had devastated the Darlington municipality, it was sold out quietly to the big group in 1995. It was well known for its big fleet of Bristol REs, which have now largely been replaced by newer buses. Seen in 1993 is No 75 (OEF 75K), working a summer Sunday service into the local countryside, at Castle Eden. *Mark Wilson*

Right:
United and its fellow North East Bus subsidiaries were for some time keen operators of the Bristol LH. Still in a livery showing little change from National Bus Company days is Plaxton-bodied dual-purpose 1801 (PTT 71R), which was new to Western National, working a Fridays-only deviation through Castle Bolton of the 159 service from Leyburn to Hawes in September 1990. *John Robinson*

Above:
North East Bus, prior to being acquired by West Midlands Travel, turned to Optare for its fleet replacement. Firstly it used midi-sized MAN-based Vectas but then placed one of the first orders for the Mercedes-Benz O.405-based Prisma. Tees & District Prisma 3021 (N521 XVN) is seen in Stockton in February 1996. *Mark Wilson*

Right:
Peace before the storm in Darlington. The date is 9 September 1991, three years before Stagecoach came to town and disrupted things, although right from deregulation the local municipality faced competition, much of it from United. Darlington had an unusual vehicle policy; it was one of the few operators which particularly liked the Seddon Pennine RU and so it got the small Huddersfield firm, Ward Bros, to built it an RU version of its Dalesman chassis, with rear Gardner engine, and then had them bodied by Wadham Stringer. The first one, 1 (A101 CVN), is seen with single-deck Roe-bodied Daimler Fleetline 55 (NHN 255K). *Terry S. Blackman*

Left:
East Yorkshire found the Routemaster a good tool for Hull in competition
with Kingston-upon-Hull City Transport; like the Scottish Bus Group
operators in Glasgow it had distinct speed advantages over one-person-
operated vehicles. East Yorkshire painted them in its old indigo and
primrose livery. However, a variety of external factors led to their
withdrawal, and recent Northern Counties-bodied Leyland Olympians
were painted in the same colours to replace them. 563 (J563 HAT) shows
the livery off to advantage during the glorious summer of 1995.
David Longbottom

Above:
West Yorkshire Road Car was for many years the dominant operator in
York. That company was split up into several bits at privatisation and
effectively disappeared. The Harrogate area become Harrogate & District,
while the York operation, York City & District, ultimately passed to
Yorkshire Rider and became Rider York. A Harrogate & District Reeve
Burgess-bodied Renault S56 passes a Rider York Leyland National 2 in
York in May 1992, with a rather anonymous Renault coming up behind.
P. J. Chancellor

15

Left:
Awkwardly-parked vehicles mean that the Leyland Lynx 205 (G297 KWY) of another successor of West Yorkshire, Keighley & District, blocks the traffic as it loads in Leeds on the Keighley service from Wetherby in June 1990. *Kevin Lane*

Above:
Sheffield has seen a great deal of competition since deregulation, though much of it has been taken over by either Mainline or Yorkshire Traction. Northern Bus is an independent active in and around Sheffield and remains so. For much of its existence it was a keen Bristol RE user, though has now changed its fleet policy. RESL6L (HRN 108N), seen near Woodsetts on 21 July 1995, was new to Fylde. *David Hatcher*

Above:
The former South Yorkshire PTE bus operator was privatised and became Mainline, and is now trying
low-floor buses. This is a Wright Crusader-bodied Volvo B6LE on Easiaccess services, with evidence of
Supertram in the foreground. *Michael Fowler*

Above:
Minibuses were used by numerous operators to stimulate demand and see off competition in the early days of deregulation. Leicester CityBus set up its 'Trippit' operation to compete in Loughborough, using new Optare CityPacers, a type which brought new style to minibuses. After a deal was struck with Trent, Trippit disappeared; this former Trippit is seen with Derby City Transport in September 1989.
B. Hayes

Left:
Following privatisation, Trent tried a number of liveries, starting with this red and silver scheme. Now it has a much brighter livery of red and cream, and remains one of the few privatised NBC companies in independent hands — at the time of writing anyway. Leyland Olympian 715 (B715 HVO) — a typical late standard NBC bus — works a local service in Kirkby in Ashfield in March 1988. *John G. Milnes*

Below left:
The Nottingham fleet was characterised by buses to its own design. However, during the 1990s it has bought more standard buses — though quite a variety of them! Seen in central Nottingham in 1996 is a Plaxton Verde-bodied Volvo B10B, with an elderly Leyland Leopard of Trent-owned Barton behind. *M. Page*

Right:
Sheffield Omnibus was another competitor in Sheffield, and this set up an operation in Nottingham — Nottingham Omnibus — using Bristol VRTs. It began in 1993, but withdrew in 1994, with City of Nottingham taking over the fleet. CJH 141V, an ex-Alder Valley Bristol VR, blocks in a Nottingham Volvo Citybus, both bound for Streetley estate. The livery was based on Preston's; most of Sheffield Omnibus's early fleet was ex-Preston Leyland Atlanteans. Sheffield Omnibus is now part of Yorkshire Traction, and in their heyday all sorts of rumours abounded about big-group involvement in the two companies. *P. J. Chancellor*

Above:
Numerous coach operators have provided bus services since deregulation.
This ex-Lincolnshire Bristol LH, XFW 951S, is seen in use by Hunts of Alford
on a local service in Skegness. *David Longbottom*

Right:
Gilbert Kinch, of Mountsorrel in Leicestershire, was well known for his high-
quality coach operations, twice winning Coach of the Year at the beginning of
the 1980s. Since deregulation Kinch became very active in local bus services in
the East Midlands — in Leicester, Loughborough and Nottingham
particularly, using an interesting fleet with several ex-London Transport
Leyland Titans. Seen in Leicester on 28 May 1988, however, is UWX 368L, an
ex-West Yorkshire Bristol RELL6G. Kinch withdrew its two Nottingham
services in 1996.
Andy Izatt

Right:
Also in Leicester is a Midland Fox Alexander-bodied Leyland Olympian, 4524 (G524 WJF), seen when new in November 1989. Behind is an Iveco minibus of the same operator and a Dennis Dominator of Leicester CityBus.
S. A. Gill

Below right:
Latterly Midland Fox has introduced a new, rather more stylish image in Leicester, using new East Lancs-bodied Scania L113s, an unusual choice of standard bus for British Bus. The fleetname carried by 2169 (N169 PUT) for this Leicester local service is Urban Fox.
John Young

Above:
Routemasters have figured with a number of operators since deregulation, crew operation being a useful selling point. Seen in Corby in 1989 is United Counties 715, former London Transport RM1820. *R. W. Cooper*

Above:
An interesting vehicle, retained by Cambus from its Eastern Counties days, was this Bristol Lodekka FLF, seen here at Yaxley in July 1988. Cambus was later split, and the Lodekka went into the Viscount half for Peterborough operations, retaining the Peterborough & District fleetname. Cambus was taken over by Stagecoach in 1995, and during 1996 the Lodekka's future looked uncertain, despite hitherto daily use in normal service.

T. K. Brookes

Above:
And here is Viscount, in the shape of two Leyland Olympians: one, on the left, with Northern Counties bodywork, the other with Leyland. They are entering Peterborough bus station in June 1991. When it was started, Viscount aimed to be the 'Marks & Spencer of the bus industry', an image tarnished when elderly Bristol VRTs were bought in from West Yorkshire, in fading red livery, to see off a competitor. *Terry S. Blackman*

Above:

Eastern Counties has had a rather strange vehicle-buying policy since privatisation, though now that it is part of FirstBus presumably this will change. In some places it has a reputation of running buses well past their 'sell-by date', notably ex-Ribble Bristol VRs pushing 25 years old, though it has bought a number of new buses, including Leyland Olympians, Dennis Darts, Volvo B6s acquired when Mainline abandoned an attack on

Ipswich, plus Dennis Lances with Northern Counties bodywork and, even more odd, 15 Dennis Javelin service buses, five with Duple bodywork and 10 — like S11 (H611 RAH) — with Plaxton Derwent bodywork. With a slightly unwell electronic destination screen it works a local service in the Great Yarmouth area, passing through Gorleston-on-Sea.
John Young

Above:
Regardless of deregulation, East Anglia has a long tradition of small independent bus operators. Chambers of Bures has taken to buying new Olympians in recent years, both Leyland and Volvo. Two of three Alexander-bodied Leylands, bought new in 1989, pass in Bures in March 1993. *John Young*

Above:
Eastern National became part of the Badgerline Group and operates a number of standard Badgerline types, including Plaxton-bodied Mercedes-Benz 709Ds like 648 (L648 MEV) at Holland-on-Sea. Under Badgerline ownership the livery was brightened up and as usual badger emblems were applied, only to be removed after the merger with GRT to form FirstBus.
Derek R. Hall

Right:
East Kent was one operator which did not stop buying new buses just because of deregulation. It continued to buy minibuses and double-deckers, finding its fleet polarised between the two types without much need for large single-deckers, other than for specific uses like the Canterbury Park-&-Ride. As well as Leyland Olympians East Kent bought 22 Mark 2 MCW Metrobuses in 1988/89. It also used a variation on its traditional colours to produce this rather handsome livery, as carried by 7761 (F761 EKM) in Lydd in July 1993, during which year East Kent succumbed to Stagecoach's big expansion drive. *G. P. Senior*

Left:
Having succumbed to Stagecoach, the group's standard types entered East Kent service. Seen in Canterbury's well-known bus station in August 1994 is an Alexander-bodied Volvo B10M shipped down from the opposite corner of England, Cumberland Motor Services. Obviously Stagecoach believes there is a rôle for large single-deckers in East Kent.
Terry S. Blackman

Below left:
Hastings & District, formed out of a split of Maidstone & District, also became part of the Stagecoach empire, but in January 1988, when this highbridge Bristol VR was trundling majestically between Rye and Appledore, amid scenery typical of the coast on the Kent and East Sussex border, it was independent.
Shaun Wallace

Right:
Before selling out to Stagecoach, Hastings & District had settled on this rather nice blue, yellow and cream livery. 558 (BKE 858T), a normal-height ex-Maidstone & District Bristol VRT, climbs Battery Hill, Fairlight, on a school service from Rye in April 1991.
Terry S. Blackman

Above:
Australian operator Westbus set up a coach operation in Britain during the 1980s, with bases in Hounslow, Middlesex and in Ashford, Kent, where the name seemed rather incongruous. The Kentish operation also began running buses; this Leyland Lynx, ex-demonstrator F608 WBV, was a typical Westbus vehicle, here passing through St Mary-in-the-Marsh in May 1991, in a scene which could only be Kent in spring. *Terry S. Blackman*

Above:
Despite domination by Stagecoach in the south and east of the county and British Bus in the north and west, Kent can still field a number of independent operators, many of them with a distinctive feel to them. One is Wealden Beeline, which operates a fascinating little fleet. One of its more unusual vehicles is this Dennis Dart coach, with Wadham Stringer's Winchester body. Wadham Stringer, not having shared greatly in the spectacular success of the Dart as a bus, tried to expand its market as a coach and built this one-off, which ran at first with Thames Transit. But the Dart really is an urban bus and did not transform well as a coach; as their name suggests, Darts are all about rapid acceleration, achieved at the expense of top speed, giving quite the wrong characteristics for coach work. Wealden has found a use for this appealing little vehicle, though: it is seen soon after acquisition in Wadhurst on a local service to Tunbridge Wells on 15 June 1994. *Eric Baldock*

Above:
Competition in Maidstone became quite acrimonious, with a group of
independents managing to get Maidstone & District hauled over the coals
by the Monopolies & Mergers Commission, after which M&D had to fight
with one arm tied behind its back. One of the conditions which arose was
that operators should not wait for more than 5min on certain stops in
central Maidstone, and soon after this ruling the writer observed one of the
independents (not the one shown here) sitting on the stand in question for
fully half an hour; perhaps they weren't quite as pure as the MMC thought.
Back in April 1993 Bygone Buses' Routemaster, former RM1677, competes
with a Maidstone & District Northern Counties-bodied Leyland Olympian
around the Park Wood housing estate, one of the more lucrative areas for
bus operation in Kent. Nowadays, with M&D in Cowie ownership,
Maidstone and district is a little more peaceful, even if the peace is a
slightly uneasy one. *Terry S. Blackman*

Above:
Odd things have happened since deregulation. Alexander Y-type-bodied Leyland Leopards may be the sort of thing you
might expect in urban Scotland, but in Tunbridge Wells? Whatever next…! Two of them, in Maidstone & District's fleet,
disturb the peace and tranquillity of that genteel town on services to and from Edenbridge. 3002/3 (TSJ 77/ 83S) were new to
Western SMT. *Terry S. Blackman*

Left:
The return of Southdown's traditional livery (or at least an approximation thereof) after privatisation was the cause of great rejoicing amongst bus enthusiasts. It was short-lived, however: now the fleet is resplendent in Stagecoach stripes and has even lost its good old Southdown name. Leyland National 2 No 133 (RUF 433X) stands in a slightly sodden Chichester bus station in October 1989. No doubt in the true traditions of Southdown service, passengers would be issued with waders to board the bus? *Andy Izatt*

Above right:
Southern Vectis still maintains a fleet of elderly Bristols as a 'heritage fleet'. In particular it uses elderly open-toppers on its service to the Needles; Bristol Lodekka LD6G 502 (MDL 952) nears the end of its journey back to Alum Bay on 15 May 1993. *Terry S. Blackman*

Below right:
Southern Vectis introduced a new livery in 1993; newly painted and looking very smart in the Island Explorer version, is all-Leyland Olympian 711 (F711 SDL) arriving at Newport on service 7A from Freshwater. *Terry S. Blackman*

Above:

The takeover of bus operators along the south coast, including Hampshire Bus and Southdown, by Stagecoach, and of London operators Selkent and East London, has led to the opportunity to update the south coast fleets — and others — with buses from London. Not that this ex-London Leyland Titan, T198, contributes to much of an improvement in age profile, though it does bring some newer technology to the Coastline fleet. Now numbered 7298 (CUL 198V), the bus came from Selkent, from which Stagecoach has eradicated the Titan with new Volvo Olympians, and works a former Southdown service from Portsmouth to Leigh Park.

Philip Lamb

Above:
In the early days of deregulation the London Transport DMS-type Daimler Fleetline was a very useful double-decker for all sorts of operators. Premature withdrawals of the type had begun in February 1979 (before London had disposed of all its RTs!) and they flooded on to the secondhand market through dealer Ensign, — then of Grays — most converted to single door. Carrying Hampshire Bus's thankfully short-lived post-NBC livery, its 1926 (OJD 245R), former DMS2245, the last of 10 bought in 1983, leaves Southampton on the operator's then main trunk route 47 to Winchester. After Stagecoach took over, the 47 passed in a complicated deal to Southampton CityBus, though following that operator's realisation that it was better off concentrating on the urban services it knew best, the route finished up with Solent Blue Line, an operator set up by Southern Vectis primarily to compete in Southampton, after deregulation.
A. L. Such

Above:

In 1996 Yellow Buses, Bournemouth, is one of the few remaining operators in local authority hands. Its position was shaken when Routemaster Bournemouth moved in on some of its best routes, but Yellow Buses saw off the threat and continues to provide a good service to Bournemouth. Bournemouth's population — and therefore Yellow Buses' ridership — is characterised by a high proportion of retired folk, and the operator specified buses with step-free entrances and lower-deck floors, long before the great low-floor bus bandwagon of the 1990s. As a result, passengers did not take kindly to a batch of Wadham Stringer-bodied Mercedes-Benz 811Ds which came in 1989. They were very quickly given the push, most of them along the coast to Brighton, where the more nimble-footed passengers don't seem to mind them on Brighton & Hove services. During their short sojourn in Bournemouth, 48 (F48 XPR) picks up in The Square.
M. G. Rainford

Yellow Buses and Wilts & Dorset cohabit quite peaceably in Bournemouth; with its strong municipality (Yellow Buses) and strong independently-owned ex-NBC company (Wilts & Dorset). Bournemouth is remarkably free of big-group operators. Yellow Buses Alexander-bodied Leyland

Fleetline 170 (MFX 170W) passes Wilts & Dorset Leyland National 3695 (PJT 272R) in Lansdowne Square in July 1989. *Kevin Lane*

Above:
Southern National and North Devon were companies split out of Western National and sold together from National Bus Company to form Cawlett Holdings in March 1988. Blending in well with its scenery at Litton Cheney in Dorset in August 1993 is Southern National Leyland National 2828

(MOD 828P), operating the Wednesdays-only service through the village between Dorchester and Bridport. The destination blind is hardly encouraging to passengers on such an infrequent service.
DWR Picture Library

Left:
Exeter can claim to be the place where high-frequency minibus operation all began in the run-up to deregulation. It was something of an experiment by the National Bus Company, which it started in 1983, and was highly successful in generating new traffic in towns (which NBC had not served terribly well) with half-hourly 'big bus' services. High frequency, penetration of housing estates with hail-&-ride operation, eliminating the need for consulting timetables or even walking to the bus stop, were contributory factors in their success, as were low running costs and the ability to employ new drivers on new wage rates and conditions. Without it there might have been many more opportunities for independent operators to give the bigger companies more of a fight; as it was NBC used its might to flood towns with minibuses in advance of deregulation, leaving little room for anyone else. Some of the earliest Ford Transits of Devon General at Exeter are lined up at the depot. Devon General was the first NBC company to be sold, to its management, led by the ebullient Harry Blundred, for whom minibuses became almost a religion. They worked superbly well in Exeter, though other parts of the empire Harry Blundred's Transit Holdings built up were perhaps not so well suited to them. In 1996 Devon General and its Bayline offshoot were sold to Stagecoach and Harry Blundred concentrated on working his magic in Australia. *M. Bailey*

Below left:
A later generation of minibus in Exeter. The Ford Transits actually confounded their critics by standing up to heavy-duty local service work remarkably well, but in the end the traffic they generated needed bigger buses offering better comfort and passenger flow. Transit Holdings developed dual-door minibuses to improve passenger flow, like this Marshall-bodied Mercedes-Benz in a distinctive new livery for Devon General's Exeter Minibus introduced in the spring of 1995.

Above:
Although Devon General built up its minibus business on Ford Transits, it was realised that larger vehicles were required for longer routes, such as Bayline's service 85 from Exeter round the cost via Dawlish to Torquay, with a running time of 1hr 20min. Reeve Burgess-bodied Mercedes-Benz 709D 49 (F749 FDV) picks up a passenger at Cockwood Harbour on the River Exe estuary, near Dawlish, on 19 June 1992. *John Robinson*

Right:
Western National was another NBC operator to be won over by the charms of the ex-London Transport DMS type; it took 38 into its fleet in 1981/82, though generally they proved fairly short-lived. They looked rather drab in NBC green, but altogether brighter in the later, post-privatisation livery. Like many places, in pre-deregulation years Western National, as the local company operator, and Plymouth City Transport had kept off each other's toes in Plymouth, but Western National decided to have a go on Plymouth local services after deregulation; some new buses were bought and the few longer-lasting DMSs were deployed on them, such as 815 (TGX 838M), former London Transport DMS838, which was working a Plymouth local service at Whitleigh on 25 April 1988.
M. Bailey

46

Left:
Deregulation did not serve the smaller, established independent operator well. While the intention was to shake the larger, public-sector operators out of their complacency, the smaller independents which had provided efficient services on a small scale all over the country were also exposed to the draught of the new era and many failed. Cornish operator Harvey's of Mousehole gave up the struggle and sold out to Western National; with it came this highly unusual Wadham Stringer-bodied Bristol LHS, which became Western National 1565

(KRL 444W), though in this view in Penzance in June 1991 it was distinguished by Blue Bus fleetnames.
John Young

Above:
Weston-super-Mare was one of the first places after Exeter to get high-frequency minibuses, with 46 Ford Transits in June 1985. Larger Mercedes-Benz minibuses came in 1992; these have Plaxton bodywork. *P. J. Chancellor*

Left:
In 1985 Bristol Omnibus launched various new liveries, including this rather radical replacement for NBC green for Bristol City Line. The following year Badgerline was split off, only for the two companies later to join up again, firstly as separate subsidiaries of the Badgerline Group and in 1995 as trading names of a combined Bristol Omnibus Company under FirstBus ownership. City Line has an impressively modern fleet; MR9622 is a Northern Counties-bodied Leyland Olympian new in 1993. *C. A. Davey*

Above:
Thamesdown Transport, based in Swindon, is still in local-authority ownership at the time of writing. Recent additions to its fleet have been Plaxton Pointer-bodied Dennis Darts; its first batch, of which 105 (K105 OMW) is a representative, in the Dartline livery carried by these buses, were short-wheelbase 8.5m vehicles.
P. J. Chancellor

Above:
In the early days of deregulation, on 15 November 1986, a Bristol VRT of Cheltenham & Gloucester, 5030 (JOU 160P), shows little sign of the changes that have already started to happen; it still carries full NBC poppy red livery as it leaves Cheltenham. *Shaun Wallace*

Right:
Oxford is one of the few places to have seen sustained head-to-head competition between two major operators, Transit Holdings having come into Oxford as Thames Transit, where its chairman Harry Blundred had been traffic manager, to compete against City of Oxford. It was in Oxford that Transit developed its dual-door minibus concept, which it later developed with dual-door Dennis Darts. Only one other British operator uses dual-door Darts in normal service — City of Oxford! Colour-coded destination blinds and local route branding for the buses are all part of the Thames Transit ethos.
Chris Morrison

Above:
Reading Mainline began operations in July 1994. It was set up by the former operations director of Reading Buses, Mike Russell, to compete against his former employer, on the basis of speed and quality. Unlike other operations using Routemasters as a competitive tool, Mainline has selected its vehicles very carefully and keeps them to a high standard, as shown by its No 5 (WLT 937), passing a Reading Buses Metrobus in the early days of Mainline, before the fleetnames appeared on the buses.

Chris Morrison

Above:

Milton Keynes is a brash new city, all concrete, glass and roundabouts. Unfortunately it has never had a swish public transport system to complement it; instead this car-dominated city was served largely by insipid-looking Mercedes-Benz minibuses following deregulation, as shown by a scruffy-looking specimen in October 1988. Milton Keynes City Bus was taken over by Cambus and thus became part of Stagecoach; however, before its new owners had a chance to give Milton Keynes bus services the pzazz they have always lacked Stagecoach had to agree to sell the business to avoid yet another reference to the Monopolies & Mergers Commission. The problem was that Milton Keynes was considered too close to its United Counties subsidiary; indeed United Counties had been the new city's first bus operator. *Kevin Lane*

Above:
Like Midland Fox, The Shires — the Cowie subsidiary once known as
Luton & District — has some East Lancs-bodied Scania Ł113s. Carrying the
Gade Valley fleetname for its local operations based in the town, SE705
(N705 EUR) is seen in Hemel Hempstead, its fleetnumber reflecting the
London Country origins of The Shires there.
Philip Lamb

Right:
Luton & District was a keen user of minibuses in the days after
deregulation, with a rather gaudy livery under the Hoppanstopper name,
at first using a particularly irritating rabbit character to promote them. He
seems to have been expunged from this Iveco, No 61, whose livery seems
rather out of place in the refined surroundings of Albury Pond, on the
Hertfordshire/Essex border, in September 1988. *Kevin Lane*

Left:

Changing direction now on our tour of Britain, we head off into South Wales. Though several privatised National Bus Company operators have disappeared through amalgamation, retrenchment etc, only one has actually failed. That was National Welsh, which collapsed in spectacular fashion in 1992, after having taken over several local municipalities. National Welsh was a great user of minibuses, under the Bustler name, with a vivid yellow livery. Most of its minibuses were Sherpas, a type usually disliked for bus work. Behind, in this view at Aberdare in 1989, is a Leyland National in the Halifax-inspired livery of Cynon Valley.
T. S. Powell

Above:

Much of National Welsh's operation finished up in the hands of a new Rhondda company, whose maroon livery reflected an older operator of the same name which had been absorbed into National Welsh in NBC days. Rhondda has a varied fleet, including various secondhand MCW Metroriders; 2120 (E640 KYW) came from London Buses in 1992 and a year later is seen at Blaenrhondda on the Valleys Line rail link to Treherbert. Alongside is a then-new Wright-bodied Dennis Dart.
John Young

Left:
Davies Bros of Pencader 209 (FIL 7131) is one of several Leyland Leopards rebodied by Willowbrook and re-registered; this one was HNU 117N, originally a Nottingham City Transport coach. It is seen near Alltwalis bound for Carmarthen from Pencader on a Bws Dyfed service in October 1993. *A. Moyes*

Above:
Roberts of Aberystwyth ran the Friday tender to Cwmrheidol until displaced by a Postbus in September 1995. Until a Freight Rover minibus took over in 1990, the regular vehicle was this splendid Plaxton Panorama-bodied AEC Reliance, RVB 411E.
A. Moyes

Above:
Some rural tendered services in Dyfed have had strongly-enhanced frequencies; the 531 east of Aberystwyth, for instance, had its weekly mileage doubled. In August 1993 Crosville Cymru Iveco MRF282 (F82 CJC) returns to Aberystwyth on the last trip from Penbontrhydybeddau.

A. Moyes

Above:
Another British Bus standard type has been Mercedes minibuses with a variety of bodywork. Crosville Cymru MMM796 (N996 CCC) has Alexander bodywork. It is seen when new in August 1995 at the former lead mines at Frongoch on the Pontrhydfendigaid circular in the Cambrian Mountains, southeast of Aberystwyth.
John Young

Above:
Gwynedd was very active in the promotion of public transport in northwest Wales prior to its abolition in 1996. Stalwart of the Bangor-Bethesda service of Purple Motors — one of a number of independents to survive in the Bangor area — was this ex-Tayside Ailsa, NSP 330R, seen at Adwy'r Nant on 1 September 1988, advertising Gwynedd's day rover ticket at £2.
A. Moyes

Right:
Bott of Abergynolwyn ran this dual-door ex-Hants & Dorset Bristol LH, RLJ 793H, on Bws Gwynedd tendered routes around Tywyn in the late 1980s; here it passes through Aberdyfi in June 1988. A requirement of vehicles used on Bws Gwynedd was that they were identified by the red front end.
A. Moyes

Left:
For many years Crosville, later Crosville Cymru, ran its Cymru Coastliner service along the North Wales coast, often with double-deck coaches; during the 1960s it had some Bristol FLF coaches for the service. Latterly Crosville Cymru used coach-seated Leyland Olympians; this one is taking on a good load in Castle Square, Caernarfon on 31 August 1988. Alongside is a Bristol VR of Express Motors. Sadly the Cymru Coastliner came to an end in 1995; now there is just a non-branded Caernarfon-Llandudno service. *A. Moyes*

Below left:
Crosville Cymru operates beyond North Wales into Chester. Bristol VR DVG513 (YMB 513W) is seen leaving Chester for a Clwyd tendered service to Connah's Quay, just over the border, on 26 June 1989. *Kevin Lane*

Right:
The English part of Crosville was bought from NBC in March 1988 by ATL, a company which disappeared from the scene soon after selling Crosville on to Drawlane only a year later. Crosville was split up, with its only remnant now being a trading name of PMT for services in parts of Cheshire. Following an alarming dark green and orange livery after privatisation, Crosville settled for this more sober livery, applied to three Sherpa minibuses seen in Chester bus station at the height of minibus operation in October 1987. *Adrian Pearson*

Above:
Chester is still quite a centre for competition, and now dark green and cream minibuses are again commonplace in the city. However, these are run by St Helens operator South Lancashire Transport, which is maybe not the most tactful trading name for use in the county town of Cheshire. Its Chester fleet comprises Alexander-bodied Dodge S56s ex-Clydeside, such as No 50 (D250 NCS). Behind is a Duple-bodied Leyland Tiger of Midland Red North, whose front appears to have been 'got at' by East Lancs. *T. E. Sutch*

Above:
Happy Al's, based in Moreton, in Wirral, is just the sort of operator Nicholas Ridley must have had in mind when he and his think-tank gurus were brewing up bus deregulation: a cheap and cheerful image with a highly distinctive appearance, a fleet of around 30 buses, most of them half-decent vehicles cast off from larger operators, providing some competition in and around Liverpool. MNS 48Y, seen in Skelhorne Street, Liverpool, in August 1995, is an ex-Kelvin Central Alexander-bodied Dennis Dominator. *K. R. Mason*

Above:
Warrington has been a scene of bitter competition: North Western and MTL both marched into town to run over Warrington Borough Transport's routes, in a move similar to that of Stagecoach in Darlington. However, Warrington proved more resilient than Darlington, and its passengers surprised the newcomers by their loyalty to the buses provided by their local-authority operator. MTL has pulled out, though at the time of writing North Western is still in there. However, Warrington has retaliated by running into Merseyside over some North Western routes; its Plaxton-bodied Dennis Dart 238 (M238 YKD) stops at Runcorn High Street bus station on the Runcorn Busway on its first day of operation on a service from Murdishaw to Liverpool, 20 March 1995. *John Robinson*

Right:
In the early days of deregulation East Midland popped up all over the place. As well as winning tendered services for London Transport and Essex County Council (resulting in odd Ongar-Mansfield services at weekends to get the buses home for maintenance!) it ran in Manchester under the Frontrunner name it used for services out of its own area. Ex-Grampian Alexander-bodied Leyland Atlantean 433 (KSA 182P) turns from Corporation Street into Cannon Street in Manchester in the early days of deregulation — probably the summer of 1987 — with Ribble buses visible in their post-deregulation livery. Now both Ribble and East Midland are Stagecoach companies, and East Midland is firmly back in its place.

Above:
MTL, having completed the privatisation of Merseybus, set out from its Merseyside area to expand. One area into which it moved was Greater Manchester, with a two-pronged attack: MTL Manchester was a new operation largely within the city of Manchester, while Lancashire Travel was a sort of latter-day Lancashire United Transport, operating mainly on the area's northern and western fringes. Heading further east than usual for Lancashire Travel is a Leyland National 2, passing through Hawkshaw on its way to Bury in October 1994. MTL later retreated from Manchester; it was losing money there and the main Manchester operators, not surprisingly, were fighting back in Merseyside. *Michael Baker*

Right:
Despite the existence of numerous independent operators in Greater Manchester, the Government was not satisfied that there was enough competition there and forced the PTA-owned Greater Manchester Buses to split into two and be sold. Perhaps the strong and vocal anti-Government stance taken by GMPTA's political masters may have had some bearing on things. After a couple of years in private hands both sold out, the northern half to FirstBus and the southern to Stagecoach, which renamed it Stagecoach Manchester. The Manchester Victoria-Southern Cemetery circular routes are considered flagships and for some time have had more modern buses than most. First signs of Stagecoach ownership were 15 new Alexander-bodied Volvo Olympians which were diverted from Stagecoach South and put into service on those routes; newly delivered 706 (N330 NPN) leaves Victoria station on 27 March 1996. *T. E. Sutch*

Above:
Trent came into the Greater Manchester area following the splitting up of the original North Western back in 1972. The Nottingham-Manchester service, operated as TransPeak, has now become part of Trent's Rainbow Routes concept, which offer a high standard of 'customer care'. New Alexander (Belfast) Q-type-bodied Volvo B10Ms, a type seldom seen outside Northern Ireland, were placed on it in January 1995. Here, 52 (M52 PRA) calls in Stockport when a few days old. *John Young*

Above:
The later style of Ford Transit was not used very much by bus operators; large quantities of the old model were bought cheap on its run-out, and by the time the new VE6 model was on stream in versions suitable for minibus conversion, operators were looking for something bigger. However, operating for Midland Red North in the Walsall area in August 1987 is Dormobile-bodied 103 (D103 CFA). *Adrian Pearson*

TAMWORTH 116
via Kingsbury

MIDLAND

SCANIA

M835 SDA

Left:
Following a period of using 1930s-style overall red Midland Red livery, Midland Red North reverted to its brighter yellow-based livery for new deliveries in 1995. A new East Lancs-bodied Scania N113, 1835 (M835 SDA), passes through Carrs Lane in Birmingham in August 1995. *Chris Morrison*

Above:
West Midlands Travel was one of the most successful operators after deregulation, partly on account of its long experience of off-bus ticket sales which it turned to competitive advantage after deregulation. In December 1986 MCW-bodied Leyland Fleetline 6998 (WDA 998T) — one of the highest-numbered buses in the fleet — waits in Wolverhampton bus station. *Shaun Wallace*

242
STOURBRIDGE
MIDLAND RED WEST
235
MIDLAND RED WEST
L235 AAB